MAKE VIRTUAL
LEARNING MATTER

How to Turn **VIRTUAL**
Classrooms into Remarkable,
Authentic Experiences for Kids

JACOB MNOOKIN
& PAUL AXTELL

simple **truths**
▶ Small books. BIG IMPACT.

Published by Simple Truths, an imprint of Sourcebooks
P.O. Box 4410, Naperville, Illinois 60567-4410
(630) 961-3900
sourcebooks.com

Printed and bound in the United States.
SB 10 9 8 7 6 5 4 3 2 1

To all parents working hard to make virtual

learning matter right now: you got this!

Contents

Choose the Perspective: This Matters

If you don't like something, change it; if you can't change it, change the way you think about it.

—MARY ENGELBREIT

Anyone who had any part in the Great Remote Teaching Experiment of 2020 will tell you that it was not great. In fact, many would tell you that it was terrible. It is rare for school administrators, teachers, students, and parents to agree on anything, and yet, most agree that remote teaching is not as effective as in-person instruction. As we prepare to start the 2020–2021 school year, however, it seems clear that virtual learning, at least in part, is here to stay.

As cities and states across the United States went into lock-down in spring 2020, the initial school closings were not the top concern for most. We all scrambled to deal with a new reality that included essentially a complete shutdown of our society. For some, that meant losing their job. For others, that meant figuring out how to do their job from home or going into work in person in an environment that potentially felt unsafe. It meant caring for family members who were sick, coping with the loss of loved ones, and connecting with those closest to us remotely, who were scared and suffering. It meant canceled weddings and remote birthday parties. And it meant teaching and learning moved from the schoolhouse to the house-house.

For schools, the scramble to move from in-person to remote teaching and learning meant that there were a lot of basic, logistical challenges that needed to be figured out. Did all the students have laptops? Did all the households have internet access? If they did have internet access, did they have sufficient bandwidth to handle potentially two parents and two children all online at the same time? Did teachers have the technological tools (and the bandwidth) they needed to teach remotely, whether that be asynchronously via recorded video lessons or through live, remote teaching?

For families, it meant figuring out who could be in what space when, with the hope that they had the quiet needed to engage in the activity before them, whether that be work, school, or downtime. It meant older siblings caring for younger siblings. And for everyone, it was hard. It was scary. And it was uncertain. In some instances, that meant families were willing to write off the last three months of the 2019–2020 school year. Education is obviously important, and yet, for many families who were struggling to adjust to the new normal, if their child didn't maximize their learning during April, May, and June, that would not be the end of the world.

And that doesn't even take into account the challenges from a teacher's perspective! They were juggling childcare with trying to teach remotely. They were learning new technological tools they were being asked to train their own students on. And they were trying to put on a brave face for their students and reassure them that everything was going to be OK, when it didn't always seem like it would be OK to them.

The unfortunate reality, however, is that learning loss, even for a relatively short period of time, has a long-lasting impact on children. Learning is cumulative, a concept perhaps most easily understood through math. Math concepts that are taught in third grade build upon the math concepts that were taught in second grade. In second grade, for example, students learn how to add and subtract within one hundred; they then learn how to work with equal groups of objects to gain foundations for multiplication. In third grade, students build upon that introductory knowledge of multiplication to learn to multiply and divide within one hundred. That's only possible if the foundational knowledge was taught in second grade.

The World Bank estimates that school closures lasting five months result in a reduction of $872 in yearly earnings for each student, which is equivalent to approximately $16,000 of lost earnings over a student's lifetime.[i] Though of course, it's not about lost earnings. The good news, however, is that it doesn't have to be that way. We do not need to throw up our collective arms and give up on virtual learning altogether. In fact, by reengaging with virtual learning, beginning with a fresh perspective that it matters in the first place can help ensure that our children are back on track, learning as they would be in a school building.

A perspective for the 2020–2021 school year: Treat each day, each lesson, and unit as though they matter

As we enter into the 2020–2021 school year, it seems inevitable that there will be some element of virtual learning for all students at some point this year. It is therefore critical for us to reset our perspective and go into the upcoming school year with the understanding that remote instruction, however imperfect, matters. We need to believe that, and we need to convey that belief to our children. This can be a great school year, and we have the power to make it so.

In addition, this is an opportunity to teach our children how to be effective working remotely, a trend that will almost certainly be critical for their long-term success, regardless of their chosen profession.

We must help our children understand that remote learning is challenging but still matters, and their determination to overcome those challenges associated with learning remotely will ultimately serve them well in life. The team at the Character Lab, who pioneered the study of grit and determination as an important attribute among successful people, notes: "There are no shortcuts. Grit predicts accomplishing challenging goals of personal significance. For example, grittier students are more likely to graduate from high school, and grittier cadets are more likely to complete their training at West Point."[ii]

Find a new mindset for virtual learning

Because it is widely understood that virtual learning is not as effective as in-person learning, the perspective that it is not effective at all has become the default understanding. If you pay attention, you'll hear people expressing, almost without realizing, a series of comments about remote instruction that are not positive.

This becomes a self-fulfilling prophecy, and remote instruction is almost doomed from the start. Here are two perspectives that provide a refreshing starting point for virtual learning. First, **virtual learning matters**—it may be the primary mode of teaching and learning this year, and for whatever grade your child is in, this is their only chance to get the most out of it that they can. Second, **choose ownership for each school day that your child attends.**

When walking around classrooms and schools, there is no shortage of inspirational quotes and motivational posters. These range from funny, to cute, to cheesy, to delightful. One of my personal favorites, however, reads, "Work Hard. Dream Big. Never Give Up." What if you made that your household mantra for your children this year as it relates to remote learning? I'm not suggesting you purchase that poster and hang it in your living room (although you certainly could!), but if you approached each day's learning with that mantra and conveyed that to your children, imagine how much more they'd be able to get out of each day's lessons.

A final perspective: This shall be

One of the fundamental variables in whether virtual learning is effective this year is how determined you are to make it so. I love the term *intention* when it means "this shall be." Intention is different from a New Year's resolution, which tends to be treated as a wish—hoped for but quickly forgotten in the demands of daily life.

Knowing you want something is not the same as being intentional about making it happen. This book shows you how to design, lead, and participate in your child's virtual learning to make a difference. The question is, will you make it happen? It's not difficult. Just take it one idea at a time, one day at a time.

TRY THIS

→ Don't give up on virtual learning because it may not be as good as in-person teaching and learning. Treat this school year, this unit, this day's lesson as if it matters.

→ Find a phrase that captures the new mindset you want for you and your children for virtual learning.

→ Collect seven phrases that communicate to your children the
importance of working hard in the face of obstacles.

Your reality is as you perceive it to be. So, it is true, that by altering our perception we can alter our reality.

—WILLIAM CONSTANTINE

1
Create Supportive Relationships

Personal relationships are the fertile soil from which all advancement, all success, all achievement in real life grows.

—BEN STEIN

In education, as in life, relationships matter. When students have a strong relationship with a teacher, it makes everything associated with teaching and learning that much easier. This idea rings true when we reflect on our own educational experience growing up. For me, my favorite teacher was Señor Amershadian, my middle school Spanish teacher. He wasn't necessarily the nicest teacher or the funniest teacher, but he was the teacher I had the best relationship with. I trusted and respected him, in part because I knew he would treat me firmly yet fairly. He didn't put up with my middle school clowning around, and he helped me understand that I had unlimited potential that I could realize if I put my mind to it.

While that is purely anecdotal, a mountain of research supports the idea that strong teacher-student relationships matter. According to an article from *Education Week*, a "Review of Educational Research analysis of 46 studies found that strong teacher-student relationships were associated in both the short- and long-term with improvements on practically every measure schools care about: higher student academic engagement, attendance, grades, fewer disruptive behaviors and suspensions, and lower school dropout rates."[iii]

In a typical school year, when students are in person in school buildings, teachers can build relationships with students naturally and through a number of interactions—both large and small—throughout the school day. Those relationships build trust between students and teachers, and in turn, they help fuel ongoing learning.

When instruction shifted from in person to remote in the spring of 2020, both parents and children could fall back on previously established relationships with their teachers. You had most likely met your child's teachers in person at some point during the 2019–2020 school year, had a personal relationship with them that grew out of those interactions, and could piggyback off of the relationship that your child had forged with them.

With many schools and school districts opening the 2020–2021 school year in a fully virtual environment, you will not have the benefit of being able to develop those relationships with your children's teachers naturally. This will inevitably make virtual learning much more challenging. Teachers won't know their students as well and won't be able to draw on their interests and personalities to help them access the learning. Students won't know their teachers as well and won't be able to indicate as easily what they need to better understand the day's lessons.

While teachers will develop plans for how to intentionally create relationships with students and families in a fully virtual setting, as the parent, you can also work to do the same with your children's teachers. To begin, try to set up a one-on-one meeting with your child's teacher. It's possible that your child's teacher was already planning on doing this, but if not, reach out and see if there is time for a virtual meet and greet.

During that meeting, come prepared to share important details about your child, including learning style, hobbies, likes and dislikes, and what the educational experience was like in the spring. Ask the teacher about plans to build relationships with students, being sure to do so in a respectful, positive way that assumes the best of intentions, and ask for periodic, one-on-one check-ins with the teacher.

You might also consider sending a note to the teacher if your child would be supportive of you doing so. In the note, you might thank them for being a teacher, tell them you look forward to seeing your child learn and grow under their guidance, and let them know that you are available if they ever want to talk. And lastly, you would appreciate any guidance on how they feel you might best support your child in learning from home. Every teacher who gets such a note will feel they have a relationship with you that they can draw upon when needed.

Conversation is at the heart of successful relationships

As you prepare for the initial meeting with your child's teacher, know that building a strong, positive relationship starts with a conversation. It is so easy to take something for granted until you don't have it—like breathing, until you suddenly can't catch your breath. Conversation is like that. Conversations are the threads that weave the fabric of our lives, and yet we don't pay attention until they're unraveling.

We work on specialized conversations, such as presentation skills, negotiating skills, sales approaches, and conflict resolution. We have not been students of paying attention to how we converse with each other. We tend to take conversations for granted. Yet relationships are created and shaped by conversations. The quality of our conversations matters.

Making conversations work

If you embrace the importance of conversation, then you can focus on what it takes to make every conversation work out as intended. The fundamental practices for effective conversation are:

1. Put the rest of the world on hold and devote yourself to the person you are with.

2 Listen in a way that encourages others to keep speaking.

3 Be aware of what you say and how you say it.

Prepare for your conversations by listing questions you want to ask or things you want the teacher to know about you or your child. Every teacher will be impressed that you are prepared.

Listening is a fine art...and often missing

As you prepare for your initial meeting with your child's teacher, you will inevitably think of a list of things you want to share with the teacher about your child. And yet, it will be just as important to listen to the teacher as it is to share details with them.

Of course, there are times when good conversation is a back-and-forth affair, even a bit chaotic. However, underlying those conversations is the notion of being able to slow down and just listen. Often that's all people need—to *be* heard, to *feel* heard. People are willing to be more expressive and honest if they sense that we are listening in an attentive way.

Be responsible for how you speak

Consider this point of view: you are responsible not only for what you say but how it is received. While this might not be expected of you, it is a high standard you can set for yourself.

TRY THIS

Arrange for a twenty-minute, one-on-one meeting with each of your children's teachers. Be sure to be respectful of the teacher's time, and know they are juggling the need to build relationships with each one of their twenty-five to thirty students and their families.

→ **Prepare for that meeting by completing the worksheet provided.**

→ During the meeting, listen longer. Speak in a way that is clear and concise.

→ Notice when commitments are made without dates, and ask for or propose a specific date.

→ After the meeting, reflect on what you said and how you said it.

No significant learning can occur without a significant relationship of mutual respect, teacher to student.

—DR. JAMES COMER

Parent-teacher kickoff meeting worksheet

❑   My child learns best when…

❑   My child's favorite subject is…

❑   My child's least favorite subject is…

❑   My child's hobbies are…

❑   My child REALLY likes…

❑   My child REALLY dislikes…

❑   Virtual learning for my child in spring 2020 was…

❑   I will view this year as a success if…

2

Decide What Matters and Why

Where my reason, imagination, or interest were not engaged, I would not or I could not learn.

—WINSTON CHURCHILL

It's safe to wager that at some point in everyone's educational career, they were made to learn something where the long-term relative importance was not immediately clear. For me, that was the Pythagorean theorem. In case you're like me and don't use the Pythagorean theorem in everyday life, you too may have forgotten this theorem, which was named after Pythagoras over two thousand years ago. Here's a quick refresher: in a right-angled triangle, the square of the hypotenuse is equal to the sum of the squares of the other two sides. This is also oftentimes written out as $a^2 + b^2 = c^2$. Remember that?

The reality is that the Pythagorean theorem is probably not particularly important in your day-to-day life, and yet, there are at least two important reasons why you should know it. The first is somewhat general: the theorem is a building block for geometry and can be used to prove a huge number of other theorems and derive other equations. We don't need to go down the rabbit hole of deciding whether all of those other theorems and equations are important to learn (at least not right now), but this relates to the idea raised in Chapter 1 that learning is cumulative. An understanding of the Pythagorean theorem allows future mathematical learning to occur, which would not be possible without it.

Now on to the second reason the Pythagorean

theorem is important. Imagine for a moment that you are at a furniture store, looking for a media console to hold your TV, and you see one that is just perfect. It fits the general aesthetic of your living room, has all of the storage space you need, and, for a limited time only, is on sale! The sale ends that very day, however, so you don't have much time to decide whether or not to buy it. If you know the measurements of your TV (and remember that TV screens are measured on the diagonal), and you know the dimensions of the opening in the media console for a TV, you'd be able to calculate whether your TV would fit using the Pythagorean theorem (and probably the calculator on your phone). Score one for Pythagoras!

Putting the imaginary media console aside for a moment, it is safe to assume that at some point this year, your child will ask you, "Why do I need to learn this?!?" We must resist the urge to reply, "Because I said so!" or "Because the teacher said so!" or worse, "I don't know! Stop bothering me!" The long-term benefit of any particular learning objective is not always clear, and that fact is exacerbated in a remote teaching and learning environment when the medium can make it seem as if the content is less important than it is.

We can hope teachers will explain how the objectives taught during a particular unit will be applicable. However, instead of solely relying on teachers to do that, we can help our children understand why the content they are learning matters, both in the moment and in the future.

Buy yourself some time

When you're hearing, "Why do I need to learn this?!?", it's likely that it will be at an inopportune moment during the day. Perhaps you are in the middle of a work meeting on Zoom asking your own, "Why...?" questions, getting dinner together, or trying to coordinate some urgent repairs that need to be done on the roof of your house. No one would blame you for, in that particular moment, responding with a curt, short response. Still, resist that instinct.

Rather, buy yourself some time by responding with something like, "The scientific method, huh? I remember learning about that. Let's find some time tonight to discuss it." That will give you some time to gather your thoughts and actually spend a moment or two considering the questions: Why is the scientific method important to learn? How do I use that in my day-to-day life?

If you're a scientist, the answer is probably relatively obvious, but for most things children are taught on a day-to-day basis, connecting the dots between what they're learning and how they will apply it is not always so straightforward.

Bring the learning home

Ideally, you will be able to use the time you bought yourself to figure out a way to extend that learning together, and perhaps there's no better concept to do that with than the scientific method. Most children constantly make observations or ask questions, such as, "My ice melts really quickly in orange juice." That's the perfect building block for a quick experiment using the scientific method:

1. **Make an observation:** "My ice melts really quickly in orange juice."

2. **Come up with a question:** "Does ice melt at different speeds depending on the liquid it is in?"

3. **Develop a hypothesis:** "I think ice melts more quickly in orange juice than it does in water."

4. **Conduct an experiment:** Bring a glass of juice and a glass of water to room temperature. Add one ice cube to each, and watch what happens. Maybe even time how long it takes for the ice to melt entirely!

5. **Record results and draw conclusions:** The ice will melt more quickly in water than in juice. Ask your child why that might be. If they don't know, Google it together! (You'll discover that the sodium/salt in juice keeps the ice from melting as quickly as it does in pure water.)

6. **Results:** Go back and discuss the original hypothesis, why they believed that initially, and how their thinking changed.

To be clear, not every question of "Why do I need to learn XYZ...?" needs to devolve into a thirty-minute science experiment, but the more often you can make connections for your child between the content they are learning virtually and how it is applicable to life both now and in the future, the stickier that learning will be, and the more likely your child will be to engage in that learning meaningfully.

TRY THIS

→ Take the time to really think about why what your child is learning matters and how they might apply that learning in their day-to-day life in the future.

→ Engage in a practical activity with your child that makes use of that learning objective. It could be Mad Libs when they're learning about parts of speech or a special experiment you plan for the weekend if they're learning about the scientific method.

The beautiful thing about learning is that no one can take it away from you.

—B. B. KING

3
Taking Care of Teachers

Never be so busy as not to think of others.

—MOTHER TERESA

For children to achieve their maximum academic potential, it is critical that they are surrounded by a single, coherent, unified voice, made up of a mixture of parents and teachers. As parents, it can be easy to forget this and devolve into an "us against them" mentality, which pits your family against the teacher. It is important to remember that teachers are people too and, as we have mentioned previously, are struggling to keep it all together as many of us are. While planning and executing lessons to their students, they are simultaneously caring for loved ones, coping with loss, worried about a spouse's lost income, dealing with internet bandwidth issues, and trying to figure out the tech needed to effectively teach their students, among many other things.

And teachers are doing all of that in an environment that does not always value them. For those of us parents who were thrust into the role of teacher in the spring of 2020, we have a newfound appreciation and understanding of how hard the job of a teacher is. As we prepare to enter into a new school year, we should continue to think about how we can take care of the teachers who are taking care of our children.

Start on a high note

Just as you may be proactively thinking about how to make the first day or first week of school feel special for your child, think about how you can also do so for your children's teachers. Unfortunately, the parent-teacher relationship is oftentimes fraught. A research report prepared by Learning Heroes notes that 71 percent of teachers are reluctant to share feedback with parents about their children because they believe, "parents blame the teacher when their child isn't performing at the appropriate level."[iv]

We can help change that dynamic by starting the year off on a positive note. Literally. Write a quick note to your children's teacher(s), letting them know how excited you are for the new school year, how challenging it must be for them to teach remotely, and how you are there for them to support them in any way you can. You probably don't have the teacher's home address, so you could inquire with a school administrator as to whether you could mail the letter to the school and have them pass it along to the teacher. Even better would be to collect four or fifteen letters from your children's classmates' parents, package them together, and mail them off to the teacher. Imagine the feeling the teacher will have when they open a package containing fifteen notes of encouragement for the upcoming school year! If coordinating feels too overwhelming, you could join the video trend, and ask fellow parents to record a quick note of encouragement as a video. You could then edit the clips together into a two-minute movie—perhaps your child could help you figure out the editing software!

A united front

It is safe to assume that at some point in this school year, your child will be frustrated with their teacher or their friend's parents will be upset with the teacher about something. It is important in these moments to give the teacher the benefit of the doubt and present a united front. That means not gossiping, not bad-mouthing the teacher to your child, not taking sides, and not undermining. Find out what is frustrating your child, and remember that their frustration is merely one side of the story. Reach out to the teacher for their perspective, being careful to do so in a kind and generous way. With both sides of the story, see if you can work with your child to overcome their frustration, or set up a meeting with the teacher if a more direct conversation is needed.

Oftentimes, you'll find that the conflict resulted from a miscommunication or misunderstanding. Or you'll discover that your child is capable of addressing the challenge on their own. You can help them work through the situation and create a plan of action by asking them a few key questions, including:

▶ "What happened from your perspective?"

▶ "What was the teacher doing when this happened?"

▶ "Try to put yourself in the teacher's shoes. What happened from their perspective?"

▶ "How do you think you could solve this?"

▶   "What could you have done differently?"

▶   "What would you have wanted the teacher to do
      differently?"

▶   "What's the plan from here?"

TRY THIS

→ Approach your child's teacher with the understanding that you're
  on the same team and working toward the same goal—helping
  your child learn and grow and develop.

→ Give your child's teacher the benefit of the doubt, and remember that they are a person too, balancing their own challenges
  associated with working from home during a pandemic.

→ Assume the best!

**Remember, there's no such thing as a
small act of kindness. Every act creates a
ripple with no logical end.**

—SCOTT ADAMS

4

Provide Structure

A champion doesn't become a champion in the ring, he's merely recognized in the ring. His "becoming" happens during his daily routine.

—JOE LOUIS

The world can be a scary, unpredictable place, filled with unknowns and uncertainty. That uncertainty can be particularly unsettling for children, whose brains are working hard to make sense of a seemingly unending number of new stimuli. One way to help students navigate the world successfully is to provide structure.

Schools often do a great job of providing students with structure and a sense of predictability. Their in-person world at school is ordered—it begins with breakfast and is followed by a morning meeting, which gives way to English class, and then math class, and then recess, etc. That predictability can have a calming effect on students and helps them to breathe a metaphorical sigh of relief, so they can more easily focus on the task at hand—learning.

When schooling moved online, a lot of those routines and structures went out the door, which added to an overall sense of anxiety among many children. It is likely that a virtual school day takes up less time than an in-person school day. If in-person school goes from 8 a.m. to 3 p.m., a virtual school day may just be from 9 a.m. to noon. How is a child supposed to fill those extra four hours? We might think our children crave that type of freedom, but the reality is their brains are likely not yet developed enough to adequately handle that amount of uncertainty.

You can help your child get the most out of virtual learning by creating a predictable routine they can follow each and every day. Using your child's virtual learning schedule as a guide and cross-referencing your own work schedule, you can then create a relatively detailed daily schedule for them. Depending upon their age, you can ask them to take on more or less responsibility for different parts of the day. You could even include them in the drafting of the base schedule!

The key components of a great daily schedule

At some schools, virtual learning can be relatively self-directed. Students are asked to log in to Google Classroom in the morning, download the day's assign-ment, and then work on that assignment on their own throughout the day, potentially accessing online resources to support them from a list the school provides. In other virtual learning settings, students will be expected to log in for a live video class led by a teacher at a particular time, and some teachers do live synchronous instruction, combined with asynchronous, pre-recorded videos. The school will provide a precise remote learning schedule, which will inform most of the day and should therefore serve as the starting point for drafting your child's daily schedule.

Once you've accounted for your child's school schedule, it is helpful to set the start and end time to each day. This certainly varies widely depending on the age of your child—a five-year-old may be up and at 'em at 6 a.m., whereas it may be a daily struggle to get your thirteen-year-old up and out of bed by 8 a.m. Even if they are previously used to getting the bus by 7:30! But with a clear start and end to the day, and using the school's virtual learning as your framework, you can fill in the additional time with:

▶ **Meals:** Depending upon the age of your children, you may be able to set the expectation that they make breakfast and lunch for themselves. You might also establish an age-appropriate clean-up routine, just as they would have at school.

▶ **Quiet time:** For some children, this may be nap time. For others, this may just be time in the afternoon to sit down with a book (or an audiobook), draw, journal, or work on a puzzle.

▶ **Active time:** Create a list of options that children can choose to engage in to ensure there is some amount of physical activity each day. This could be going for a walk or a bike ride in your neighborhood (or a hike in the woods if you have access), walking the dog, or raking leaves. Perhaps you could even make this a family activity. If you can arrange your work schedule to allow you to take a break in the middle of the day, perhaps the whole family can get their blood flowing together!

▶ **Chores:** If your family already splits chores, this time can just be dedicated to your children completing their daily chores. If you don't have one, create a list of ways that they can contribute to the household and allow them to choose. Things like unloading the dishwasher, folding their laundry, or feeding the dog can help fill the day and take some of the pressure off of you! Take advantage of the times when children are small and want to help. Yes, it takes longer, and the results might not be pretty, but you're building skills and creating the opportunity for kids to take responsibility. For older kids, ask for what you want and let them know you need their support. And for sure, thank them afterward.

▶ **Screen time:** While many families try to limit the amount of screen time their children engage in every day, the reality is, with so many hours in the day to fill, it may be a necessity. Schedule screen time for later in the day, making clear that it is earned only when they have completed their academic work and chores. With YouTube and various online learning channels, there is also the possibility of making this screen time an extension of their academic pursuits. This screen time could also be used as an opportunity to extend active time by following an online yoga or bodyweight movement routine.

▶ **Family time:** Cap the day with dinner and some type of family activity to help you set boundaries for your own work-from-home schedule, such as playing a board game, reading aloud, watching a TV show, or taking a neighborhood walk.

Once you've drafted a reasonable schedule, present it to your child for their input and feedback. "What do you think?" can be a powerful question if asked authentically.

Of course, it takes time to ask; it's easier to just command. But after some age, maybe six or eight, commanding just won't deliver the engagement and results you want. In addition to being responsible for certain parts of the day, it's also useful to keep asking for input from your kids. Being involved or consulted even when they don't get to decide is important. By asking, "What do you think?", you are communicating a variety of messages that enable children to be resilient in a world that is at times difficult to navigate: they are loved, they have choices, they have influence with the family, they add value to the family, and they are included in family conversations.

TRY THIS

→ Create a daily schedule for your children, centered around the school's virtual learning schedule.

→ Provide them with some element of choice throughout the day.

→ Once you've drafted the daily schedule, share it with your child for feedback. Make as many changes as they suggest as long as the outcomes are achieved.

Goals don't make things happen, systems do.

—SCOTT ADAMS

Virtual learning sample schedule

Morning

TIME	ACTIVITY	NOTES
8:00 a.m.–10:00 a.m.	Wake up, breakfast, clean up, and prepare for the day	❑ Shower ❑ Brush teeth
10:00 a.m.–10:30 a.m.	ELA	
10:35 a.m.–11:05 a.m.	Math	
11:10 a.m.–11:40 a.m.	Science	

Afternoon

TIME	ACTIVITY	NOTES
11:45 a.m.–12:15 p.m.	Projects	
12:20 p.m.–1:00 p.m.	Lunchtime	❑ Help clean up
1:00 p.m.–2:30 p.m.	Quiet time	Options include reading, listening to an audiobook, working on a puzzle, drawing, or free write.
2:30 p.m.–4:30 p.m.	Active time	Everyone participates! Options include going for a hike, walking the dog, or riding bikes.

Evening

TIME	ACTIVITY	NOTES
4:30 p.m.–5:00 p.m.	Chores	
5:00 p.m.–6:00 p.m.	Screen time	All academics and chores must be completed in order to earn screen time.
6:00 p.m.–9:00 p.m.	Dinner and family time	❏ Wash dishes ❏ Wipe down kitchen table ❏ Put away leftovers ❏ Sweep kitchen floor
9:00 p.m.	Bed time	❏ Wash face ❏ Floss ❏ Brush teeth ❏ Read

5

Set Expectations

High achievement always takes place in the framework of high expectations.

—CHARLES KETTERING

When the stay-at-home orders were first implemented in New York in April 2020, I was quick to make allowances for myself in ways that I never would have previously. I used to be fairly rigid as it related to many aspects of my day-to-day routine—up at 6 a.m., working out by 6:30 a.m., starting work by 8 a.m., no dessert on weeknights, and so on. But as the nightly news grew bleaker and bleaker, I found myself giving myself a break. I'd sleep until 7:30 a.m., work out every other day, and somehow a box of Cap'n Crunch made its way into my cupboard, a sugary cereal I hadn't enjoyed since I was ten years old. It was little consolation to know that I wasn't alone in my junk food vice, as sales of Goldfish crackers were up 23 percent in April 2020.[v]

Just as we were more forgiving of many of our own routines, we were also oftentimes more lax in the ways we parented our children. We tolerated more mess in bedrooms, allowed more screen time, and took a more laissez-faire approach with schoolwork. However, as the pandemic now stretches far past the spring with no clear end in sight, we must adjust to this new normal and create new expectations for ourselves and our children. While that may or may not include Cap'n Crunch in the cupboard, it absolutely must include clear expectations for how our children engage with virtual learning.

Key virtual learning considerations

Where

Space for learning can be a particular challenge for many families when several family members are simultaneously working from home. For a family with two working parents and two school-aged children, it seems likely that at some points during the day, all four will have to be logged onto the internet at the same time. It is also just as likely that there aren't four relatively private and quiet spaces for each person to log on from or an equal number of devices. That has forced families to come up with creative solutions and, in some instances, has led to awkward classroom Zooms. The internet is now filled with (often hilarious, if not cringeworthy) videos of virtual learning Zooms gone wrong. That is a club you and your family most certainly do not want to join. To avoid that, designate a specific location for each child to log in from. In a best-case scenario, this includes a desk or table, but even if that is not possible, you can still set some clear expectations:

▶ Sit upright (not lying down on the couch or in bed).

▶ Be thoughtful of who may be coming in and out of the space. We are now using our homes in ways that we didn't need to previously. In addition to being classrooms and work offices, they are also our movie theaters, restaurants, coffee shops, and gyms—sometimes simultaneously. Make sure your children are in a space where they won't suddenly be interrupted by your daily stretching routine.

▶ Be mindful of the background. When I was growing up, my family had a few paintings that were most definitely art but also included nudity. Best not to take a seat directly in front of such paintings for the daily Zoom class. A bookcase, a blank wall, or a cabinet would all work well. Worst case, do a quick search for "Basic Zoom Background," find one that looks reasonable, download that, and set that as your child's background.

For extra credit, and if time, space, and budget allow, you could work to make a corner of your house or apartment your child's schoolroom. Your child could help you design and personalize it, and this could become a special space, both practical and comfortable. There could be homemade artwork that your child creates and hangs, which serves as their unique Zoom background. There could be a little nook filled with cozy pillows that serves as their space for independent reading. And there could be a small cart, filled with the supplies they'd need throughout the day, including paper, colored pencils, scissors, glue, and more.

How

If the exponential growth in sales of sweatpants is any indication, dress codes have definitely become more casual as the world has shifted to working and learning from home. Even if the rules around what we wear have become more lax, you can still set some expectations for your children. This is, after all, their job in many ways, and you can convey to them the importance of taking the work seriously, in part, at least, through how they show up for it. While that does not necessarily mean they need to wear a button-down shirt tucked into slacks, it should mean no pajamas. The particular expectations you set for your child are not as important as setting them in the first place. By telling your child that how they show up matters, you convey the sense that learning matters and is something to be taken seriously.

In addition, it's worth talking about how they show up for online learning outside of what they wear. Remote teaching is really hard for teachers and puts a strain on them as they work to juggle their own childcare, the day-to-day responsibilities of being an adult, and teaching over the internet from home. They are working hard to think of creative ways to engage students remotely, create positive relationships, and make the learning come to life. Support the teachers, thereby benefiting your child's learning, by communicating these simple expectations to your children:

▶ **Set your Zoom screen name as your actual name.** This is not the time to try to make your classmates laugh by typing your name as "New York Knicks #1 Fan."

▶ **Default to video on and microphone muted.** Particularly for live virtual classes, it is important for the teacher to be able to see their students. To that end, it is important to keep the video on. If there are twenty or twenty-five or thirty students in the class, however, it is just as important that students keep themselves muted, unless the teacher directs otherwise. That will ensure that the combined background noises from thirty different spaces don't drown out the lesson. There may be times when the teacher asks the class to unmute as a whole, or may ask specific students to unmute at particular times, but defaulting to video on and microphone muted is a good starting place.

▶ **Be fully present.** With cell phones, tablets, laptops, and video game consoles, many kids today have access to more technology than we could have dreamed of when we were growing up. There is a time and a place for each of these gadgets, but that time and place is not during remote learning (unless it is the medium through which remote teaching is being delivered, like a tablet or laptop). So put the phone away, turn off Netflix, close out the other tabs on the internet browser, and text with your friends when class is over. The relatively limited time you have with your teacher should be focused on the task at hand—learning that day's objective.

TRY THIS

→ Create expectations collaboratively with your children.

→ Set clear expectations for *where* your children should be engaging in virtual learning.

→ Set clear expectations for *how* your children should be engaging in virtual learning. This can include their attire as well as what they should and should not do during live virtual classes.

The quality of our expectations determines the quality of our action.

—JEAN-BAPTISTE ANDRÉ GODIN

6

Know the Tools

Any sufficiently advanced technology is indistinguishable from magic.

—ARTHUR C. CLARKE

The technological tools that we have at our disposal are constantly changing, evolving, and being upgraded. Whether you're dealing with hardware or software, it is hard to keep track of it all. Just when we felt we understood what Facebook was and how to monitor our children's usage of it, Instagram came along. Once we figured that out, Snapchat quickly became the new social media site of choice among teens. And just like that, the only social media site that seems to matter is TikTok.

Just as social media is ever changing, so are the tools we use to work and learn remotely. It's hard to believe that in 2009—just eleven years ago—the iPad didn't even exist, yet nowadays, tablets are a ubiquitous part of our virtual work and learning environments. As more and more workplaces make a shift to remote work and virtual learning continues into the 2020–2021 school year, the tools we utilize to make these endeavors not just possible but productive will inevitably change. That said, a few tools have become relatively standard, and it would serve you well to familiarize yourself with those. Doing so will allow you to better support your child with any tech-related issues that may arise, periodically monitor their usage, and make sure they are using the tools appropriately.

The tools

Google Classroom

Google has quickly moved beyond being a simple search engine to take over many parts of our digital lives. It has the most widely used email service, which links to its popular calendar, all of which lives within the G Suite of online services. Those services include online-accessible software like Google Docs and Google Sheets, which compete with Microsoft's Word and Excel and allow people to collaborate relatively easily both virtually and in real time.

Google Classroom is essentially a school-focused platform that incorporates Google's G Suite of products, including Google Docs, Google Sheets, and Google Slides, in a way that allows teachers to manage the flow of information for their classroom virtually. If your child's school utilizes Google Classroom, they'll receive an invitation to "join" a classroom. Once in that classroom, their teacher will be able to post announcements, assignments, quizzes, and more. Students can submit homework assignments via Google Classroom through various means, and teachers, in turn, have various ways of providing feedback on those assignments, including through a rubric feature. In addition, Google Classroom offers the opportunity for video conferencing through Google Meet. Students can work together outside of class using the shared screen function.

As more and more of our lives are lived online these days, privacy is a concern and should be particularly examined as it relates to your children and their virtual learning. Google as a company has a mixed reputation when it comes to online privacy, so privacy concerns related to Google Classroom are to be expected. You can adjust the privacy settings from their Google Account page, assuming they use their personal Gmail account to log in to Google Classroom. Particular settings to look into are on the Personal Info, Data and Personalization, and People and Sharing pages. You may also want to help your children adjust their notification settings so their inbox is not flooded with each due date, post, and comment.

Zoom

Seven months into the global pandemic, it's likely that many of us are familiar (if not overly familiar) with Zoom. We've used it for work, virtual happy hours, birthdays, weddings, and even funerals. At its best, it has allowed us to stay connected during a time when we would otherwise be isolated, but like everything, it is not perfect. There are privacy concerns and previously unimagined troubles like "Zoombombing." As previously mentioned, a beneficial setup for navigating Zoom should include a neutral background, having the video on and the microphone muted at the start of class, and setting up their screen name to be their actual name.

Zoom does have a chat feature, which the teacher can either enable or disable. If enabled, your children may be able to send private chats to their friends in the class, which are not visible to the teacher. Review expectations for if/when they should send private chats to their friends and classmates when that option is available.

Once in a live-streamed class through Zoom, your child will have the option of "Speaker View," where the video of whoever is speaking is front and center or "Gallery View," where they can see a small video of all of the participants. It's also possible to "Pin" a video so that that person's video stays front and center regardless of who is talking. When a teacher is presenting new information, it is probably best to pin that video from Speaker View. If the class is engaging in a discussion, however, it may make more sense to switch to Gallery View.

One thing many of us can personally attest to is that long periods of time spent on Zoom can be draining in a way that interacting in person is not. Talk to your child's teacher and school administrators about how much time they expect students to be on Zoom throughout the day, and then be intentional about trying to limit the time spent on it and other screens outside of that.

From online to offline

It is worth remembering that online tools are a means and not an end unto themselves. Zoom and Google Classroom allow for remote instruction to happen but should be supplemented by authentic, real-world applications. Without the in-person school environment, this may be up to you, as the parent, to recreate. You can draw from online resources such as Pinterest, YouTube, or even simple Google searches to help you find experiments, craft projects, or books that can help extend the learning beyond Zoom and Google Classroom.

The new and unknown

While Google Classroom and Zoom are two of the most popular tools used by schools to deliver virtual learning, they are by no means the only ones, and inevitably, new ones are being created that may upend everything. In that way, it is important to get brought up to speed quickly when the school deploys new technology. There are many different websites that do a great job of providing accessible overviews for parents of popular and emerging online technology. Sites like Common Sense Media (commonsensemedia.org) can provide an overview of the new and widely used tech and include considerations regarding privacy and monitoring usage.

When tech issues arise, such as audio or video challenges, often the best option is to log off, reboot the device, and try logging back in. If there are many people simultaneously logged onto the internet and engaging in data-heavy activities, it may cause a slowdown that makes Zoom untenable. You can check your internet's download speeds at speedtest.net. According to Zoom, you need a minimum 1 Mbps download speed (or up to 3.0 Mbps upload and download speeds for high resolution) for group calls.[vi] If you find your internet is not up to the task, it is worth calling your internet service provider to inquire about available options.

TRY THIS

→ Find out from your child's teacher or school what tools they will rely on to deliver virtual instruction. Take some time to learn about those tools so you can support your child when issues arise and also monitor their usage of those tools.

→ Use online resources to create opportunities to extend learning, and take it offline from Zoom and Google Classroom to at-home science and craft projects.

→ Many kids are more tech savvy than we realize. If your child is a digital native, have them teach the rest of the family how to make the most out of the technology!

Knowing is half the battle.

—G.I. JOE

7

Participating in Virtual Learning to Learn

Wherever you are, be all there.

—JIM ELLIOT

For those of us fortunate enough to be able to transition to working from home, there have certainly been some benefits. With a non-existent commute time, there is more time in the day; lunch breaks can now consist of a home-cooked meal instead of a cold turkey sandwich; relaxed dress codes often means business casual has become *casual* casual. For many, it might seem unequivocally positive that some employers have announced they will allow employees to work from home for the foreseeable future—and possibly forever. But we must still reckon with the fact that some aspects of working in an office with our colleagues are advantageous and take intentional planning to replicate in a remote setting.

The social bonds that are formed in person are more challenging to maintain when working remotely. The serendipitous conversations that happened when passing a colleague's desk or office, which then led to an exciting new project or collaboration, are now no longer possible, so we have figured out ways to intentionally engage with each other remotely. Managers host coffee breaks on Zoom, where people can drop by to chat; coworkers schedule virtual lunch breaks to catch up. Message apps like Slack allow coworkers to stay in relatively frequent communication. And Zoom happy hours keep the good times rolling after work ends.

But each of these examples represents an intentional

practice that we must take in order to make up for what is lost by working virtually. Meaningfully participating in work or school remotely does not come naturally to many of us, so as parents, we must teach our children how to get the most out of virtual learning. Many of the topics covered in previous chapters, including setting a clear daily schedule, helping your child understand the importance of the content, and setting clear expectations will certainly help. But there are additional measures you can take to proactively teach your child—and yourself—to get the most out of virtual learning.

Teach your child

Be actively engaged

The most important thing students can do to get the most out of virtual learning is to be an active participant. This means sitting upright and being actively engaged in the lesson, free from distractions, whether those be electronic (their cell phone with the nearly irresistible allure of TikTok) or familial (the adorable dog staring at them doe-eyed with a ball in its mouth, begging to go play catch). Depending on the room, the potential distractions are almost endless: TV, baseballs, instruments, costumes, younger siblings, work for a different class, or other tabs on the screen since the laptop is at their fingertips anyway.

Ask for help

Just as it is potentially harder for serendipitous conversations to take place when working remotely, it is also harder for students to ask questions when learning virtually. If a class is being held synchronously over Zoom, your child should take advantage of the tools the teacher has enabled, which may include the Q&A button, the chat box, or the "Raise Hand" feature. You can also find out from the teacher what children should do if they still have a question after the lesson. Each teacher will have a different preference. Send an email?

Post a comment on Google Classroom? Ask three (friends) before me?

Especially when content is being delivered asynchronously or via Google Classroom, it's likely the teacher will offer scheduled opportunities for students to get support. This may be through virtual office hours or through an open invitation for students to set up a one-on-one meeting with the teacher. Rely on the relationship you have been developing with your child's teacher to find out what opportunities are available for getting extra help, and encourage your child to take advantage of those opportunities. You can also connect your child with a classmate through Zoom, Facetime, or Google Meet to allow them to help each other and work together as they would have in person.

Be looking for something

Of course, most of your child's attention needs to be on listening to the teacher and working to understand the lesson. But their minds are fast—freaky fast—so we can also give their minds another job. For a while, my daughter thought she wasn't smart. Her reasoning was based on two things: other kids raised their hands faster in class, and sometimes she didn't understand what the teacher said. Rather than try to convince her she was smart, we asked Amy to keep track of who raised their hands in which classes. Her data came back:

▶ Some kids never raise their hands.

▶ Some kids raise their hands even when they don't know the answers.

▶ Some kids raise their hands in some classes but not in others.

▶ And I raise my hand when I do my homework. Breakthrough!

What your child might look for:

► All the times they don't understand what the teacher said.

► New things they learn about their classmates.

► How many times each week they ask a question or contribute to a discussion.

► Things they think their parents should know.

Teach yourself

Be actively engaged

Just as it is important for your children to engage in virtual learning free from distractions, in the moments when you are helping them, you must also be free from distractions. If you have time set aside in the afternoon to help your children with their homework or to review the lessons they learned throughout the day, participate in those fully. Make sure your own screens are put away, and mentally clock out of your own work. You are an important model for your child on how to meaningfully participate and engage in activities. Doing so can help you really understand what your children are learning and offer ways to help them.

Don't overparent

Don't solve every problem for your children. The desire to protect them is a natural one. Sometimes, however, parents can take that tendency too far and proactively try to solve so many potential issues for their children that there aren't any mistakes for them to learn from. Children need to learn how to advocate for themselves and how to speak up when something isn't right. When we solve problems for our children, we limit their ability to learn those essential skills. Numerous research studies have shown the potentially negative effects of "helicopter parenting." One such study found that "children raised by overinvolved or helicopter parents fail to develop important competencies such as time management and coping skills. These children show less creativity, spontaneity, enjoyment, and initiative in their spare time; are less attentive to the emotions of others; have less self-confidence, self-respect, life fulfillment, and self-acceptance; are more prone to anxiety, depression, and stress; and cannot apply life skills on their own."[vii] So as your children engage in virtual learning, know that not everything will be perfect, and inevitably, things will go wrong. There are moments when you will need to step in and help, but there are also moments when they should be trusted to figure it out for themselves.

TRY THIS

→ Limit outside distractions, so your children can be actively engaged in virtual learning.

→ Help your children ask for help—use the "Raise Hand" feature during a Zoom class, sign up for office hours with their teacher, or email their teacher questions.

→ Be actively engaged yourself when working with your children on their schoolwork.

→ Let your children make mistakes, learn from those mistakes, and move forward in a positive way.

Thirty years ago my older brother, who was ten years old at the time, was trying to get a report on birds written that he'd had three months to write. It was due the next day. We were out at our family cabin in Bolinas, and he was at the kitchen table close to tears, surrounded by binder paper and pencils and unopened books on birds, immobilized by the hugeness of the task ahead. Then my father sat down beside him, put his arm around my brother's shoulder, and said, "Bird by bird, buddy. Just take it bird by bird."

—ANNE LAMOTT

8

Maintain Social Bonds

Wishing to be friends is quick work, but friendship is a slow-ripening fruit.

—ARISTOTLE

When you think about your experiences in school, whether that be K–12 or in college, you will undoubtedly remember some particular academic lessons, such as the lesson about fact vs. opinion or the lesson on fractions where you got to eat a slice of pizza. But you also probably remember the elation you felt when you won a race in P.E. Or the despair you felt in elementary school when you got into your first fight with your best friend. Or the pride you felt when your team came in second in the school-wide science fair. Or you remember feeling badly for a student who was being teased. Perhaps you were the one being teased or were the teaser yourself. And you remember your first crush.

The lessons learned at school are not a purely academic pursuit but also a social one. It is at school that we learn to move from parallel play to cooperative play. We learn how our actions impact a broader community. We learn how great it feels to receive a compliment and how it feels even better to give one.

The concerns around lost learning associated with virtual instruction are real and valid but often focus solely on academic achievement. Our children, however, are also losing out on the incredibly important socialization learned at school. Therefore, it is incumbent upon us to think about how we can help our students forge new friendships and maintain current ones in a remote setting.

Forge new friendships

Classmates

It is certainly not as natural to create new friendships with classmates in a virtual setting. There aren't necessarily opportunities to get to know someone in a hallway, outside at recess, when you're settling into class, or during lunch—all of the in-between times at a school when friendships are started. But it is still possible. Encourage your child to listen during synchronous video lessons for what they can learn about others. Classmates will share things that give insight into their personality and hobbies, perhaps what they did over the weekend or their love of a particular video game. Armed with information, encourage your child to reach out to classmates, and see if they want to set up a time to do something together. Depending on the age, this could be that shared video game they both love or a shared craft project over Zoom. Maybe even a bike ride.

Pen pals

You could also help your child forge a new friendship that is slightly farther flung. Perhaps you studied abroad in college, and your host brother or sister also has a family now. Why not see if they are open to being a pen pal with your child? They can exchange letters once a month and develop a friendship while learning about a new culture and expanding their horizon. If you don't know of anyone you can set your child up with, perhaps you could find someone through a Facebook group or a website like globalpenfriends.com.

Maintain friendships

Virtual options

Just as many of us have gotten creative in the ways we maintain our friendships virtually, so too can your children. In some ways, many kids are better equipped to manage this than we are—they've grown up using text messaging and communicating (constantly) with their friends through social networks. But encourage your children to engage with friends in new and different ways. This could be through a shared activity app like Caribu, which lets you read books, color pages, or finish mazes together virtually. Or it could be through a virtual cooking class that they take together. One great thing about having so much of our lives conducted online is that it has opened up a new world of opportunities for classes and activities that were previously only accessible in person.

In-person play dates

Just as nothing can fully take the place of in-person instruction, nothing can fully take the place of an in-person play date. Reach out to the parents of your child's close friends, and see if they are open to arranging an in-person play date. It's helpful to negotiate all of the health and safety protocols in advance. Will your children need to wear a mask? Will they need to maintain social distance? Whatever you're comfortable with and feel is best for your family and circumstances, make that clear to avoid any awkwardness once the play date begins. Meeting at a local park can be a great way for children to get some fresh air, get their blood flowing, burn off some extra energy, and see their friends!

Make it a family affair

Maintaining friendships in a remote setting is not just a challenge for our kids but for parents as well. In some ways we may have become more connected—arranging Zoom happy hours with a group of friends from college that we normally only talk to once or twice a year. But Zoom after Zoom takes its toll, and many people are finding themselves avoiding additional screen time outside of the requirements of work. This is a great opportunity for you to make the effort to maintain your relationships a family affair. Set aside twenty minutes once a week when the entire family comes together around a table to write one card to a friend, godparent, grandparent, aunt, uncle, or cousin. You can make this an exciting ritual by:

▶ Purchasing your children personalized stationery

▶ Letting them designate a favorite writing instrument they can use for just such an occasion

▶ Letting them pick out a sheet of stamps they are excited by at usps.com. There are always new stamps that the U.S. Post Office puts out (at time of print, my personal favorite is a Bugs Bunny stamp, followed closely by a stamp celebrating the moon landing in 1969).

In addition to writing letters together, the family can spend time together doing a multitude of community-building but socially distant activities. Perhaps you take some time over the weekend to make and deliver some baked goods for your neighbors. Or gather up canned goods and drop them off at a food pantry. There are also people who reach out on Facebook or Nextdoor asking for volunteers to talk with or otherwise help out local seniors. You can take your child grocery shopping for a senior who isn't able to go shopping or volunteer at a local animal shelter to play with or walk dogs. Each of these activities will help your children meet new people and develop and hone the social skills that they might otherwise be learning at school.

Notice who is on the outside

I remember taking my five-year-old granddaughter, Abigail, to her first day of school. We got there, and all the kids were outside playing. "I don't know anybody. Who can I play with?" she asked softly. "Well, do you see any other kids who don't have anyone to play with?" I asked. "That boy over there is all alone. That girl is playing by herself. Oh, I'm going to go ask that girl by the swings to play with me." And off she went. In the short term, I was helping Abigail find someone to play with. For the long term, though, this was about teaching her to notice who is on the outside. Inviting people to play or to share their story in class is a valuable skill and an important theme in life. If you have a quiet child, it can connect them to others. If you have an outgoing child, they can be a gift to others.

TRY THIS

→ Encourage your children to intentionally identify opportunities to share in hobbies or interests with new classmates.

→ Sign up your children and one of their friends for a virtual cooking class (or some other online opportunity).

→ Set aside time over the weekend when the entire family can get together to strengthen social bonds with the broader community, whether that be through writing an old-fashioned card to a friend or making some home-baked goods for your neighbors.

Be slow to fall into friendship; but when thou art in, continue firm and constant.

—SOCRATES

CONCLUSION
Celebrate Success

The more you praise and celebrate your life, the more there is in life to celebrate.

—OPRAH WINFREY

We have each faced adversity in different ways in the past few months. People have lost jobs and loved ones. The day-to-day routines we took for granted, such as going grocery shopping or to the gym, were complicated if not halted altogether. We have canceled birthday parties and postponed weddings. We have taken up new hobbies and begun cooking more. And we have worked to conduct more and more of our lives in our homes, seated in front of a computer screen.

These are challenging times. But in these moments of struggle, we have learned a lot. We have learned that we can do with less. We have learned that there were friendships that we took for granted. And we learned that there are an infinite number of home improvement projects to tackle when forced to stay inside for an extended period of time.

Just as we have moved more of our lives online, learning has moved from the schoolhouse to the computer. While there is a lot of promise and potential in remote learning, as has previously been discussed, it is not a perfect substitute for in-person instruction. If our schools will rely on remote instruction for some portion of this upcoming academic year, we cannot simply throw up our hands and write it off. It is critical that our children get as much out of their virtual learning as possible, as it will have a long-term impact on future academic achievement.

Hopefully the tips and suggestions presented in previous chapters have helped your family find some harmony and open more learning opportunities for your children. Ideally, you have:

► Conveyed to your children that this year, and the virtual learning that it contains, is important

► Forged positive relationships with your children's teachers

► Helped your children understand why what they are learning is important

► Provided them with structure and routine

► Set expectations for how they engage in virtual learning

► Familiarized yourself with the tools they rely on for virtual learning

► Supported your child to get as much out of remote offerings as possible

► Helped them maintain, if not build, social bonds

Now it is time to celebrate!

The small successes

For accomplishing all of that, you and your child deserve to celebrate that success. This is not about giving your children a participation trophy every time they try. Rather, this is about acknowledging that these times are unusual and stressful, and we all appreciate some positivity to help motivate us. One way you can do this is by modifying traditions you used to keep when your children went into an actual school building. Perhaps you used to write a note and slip it into their lunch box every Monday. While they may not be taking a lunch box to school anymore, you can still write them encouraging notes! When they're eating lunch at home, tape the note to the bottom of their lunch plate, or place it on the same page as the bookmark they're using to keep place in the book they're reading, or tape it to the bathroom mirror.

You can also create a tradition whereby every night at dinner, each person shares one thing they are grateful for. This can help each of us to acknowledge and remember that no matter how hard things are, we each have many blessings to celebrate. The idea of gratitude is particularly important for children to learn. According to the Character Lab, "Grateful people are happier and more fulfilled. And gratitude leads you to be nicer to other people: more cooperative, patient, and trusting."[viii] When the whole family participates in expressing daily gratitude, your children get a powerful model they can use to frame the way they approach each new day.

Schools are usually very creative when it comes to celebrating students. For example, a school might allow for a five minute Atten-Dance dance party during the morning meeting for students who had perfect attendance in the previous month. What age-appropriate rituals can you create for your child to help them celebrate their small wins along the way? A five-minute dance party on the first day of the new month could be a great way to acknowledge their efforts over the previous month.

The large successes

An Atten-Dance, an encouraging note on a Monday, and daily gratitude practice are great ways to keep a positive outlook during virtual learning and celebrate the small wins. In addition, there are important, more significant milestones that should be honored as well. While your child's commute to their first day of the new academic year might consist entirely of walking from their bedroom to the living room, you can still make it the momentous event you would have if they had been taking a bus. Make their favorite breakfast to celebrate the first day of school, have them get dressed up, and take their picture on your front steps as you would have for any other school year.

Another way that schools acknowledge the hard work of their students is by displaying student work prominently for other classmates to see. This is often done on a bulletin board in the back of a classroom or in the hallway. Perhaps you don't have a bulletin board in your home's hallway, but you can create a beautiful display to honor your children's hard work, beyond the usual hanging of pictures on the refrigerator. You could purchase 8.5 x 11-inch picture frames and replace some of the photos you have hanging in the front hallway with work your children are particularly proud of. Perhaps your child could create and decorate their own bulletin board out of cardboard, and use it as their backdrop for their virtual classes.

TRY THIS

→ Make a list of the encouraging school-related rituals you used to hold for your children, and figure out how to adapt them to a virtual setting.

→ Start a family-wide daily gratitude practice.

→ Identify a prominent place in your house where you can display your children's work, and plan to do so in a grand way.

Remember to celebrate milestones as you prepare for the road ahead.

—NELSON MANDELA

Endnotes

i   "COVID-19 Could Lead to Permanent Loss in Learning and Trillions of Dollars in Lost Earnings," The World Bank, June 18, 2020, https://www.worldbank.org/en/news/press-release/2020/06/18/covid-19-could-lead-to-permanent-loss-in-learning-and-trillions-of-dollars-in-lost-earnings.

ii   "Grit," Character Lab, https://characterlab.org/playbooks/grit/.

iii Sarah D. Sparks, "Why Teacher-Student Relationships Matter," *Education Week*, March 12, 2019, https://www.edweek.org/ew/articles/2019/03/13/why-teacher-student-relationships-matter.html#:~:text=A%20Review%20of%20Educational%20Research,fewer%20disruptive%20behaviors%20and%20suspensions%2C.

iv "Report Cards Sit at the Center of the Disconnect," Learning Heroes, December 2018, "Parents 2018: Going Beyond Good

Grades," https://r50gh2ss1ic2mww8s3uvjvq1-wpengine.netdna
-ssl.com/wp-content/uploads/2018/12/2018_Research_Report
-final_WEB.pdf.

v   Julie Creswell, "'I Just Need the Comfort': Processed Foods
Make a Pandemic Comeback," *New York Times*, April 7, 2020,
https://www.nytimes.com/2020/04/07/business/coronavirus-pro
cessed-foods.html.

vi   "System Requirements," accessed September 3, 2020, https://
support.zoom.us/hc/en-us/articles/201362023-System-require
ments-for-Windows-macOS-and-Linux.

vii   Ilkay Ulutas, "The Impact of Helicopter Parenting on the Social
Connectedness and Anxiety Level of University Students,"
2014, https://www.researchgate.net/publication/309492949
_The_impact_of_helicopter_parenting_on_the_social_connected
ness_and_anxiety_level_of_university_students.

viii   "Gratitude," Character Lab, https://characterlab.org/playbooks
/gratitude/.

Acknowledgments

Jacob Mnookin

I have to start by thanking my incredible wife, Isabel. She is a middle school math teacher, which has to be one of the hardest jobs in the world. Her dedication to her job and her students is inspiring, and the care with which she approaches remote learning formed the backbone of much of this book. While preparing for the upcoming school year, she read early drafts of this book and gave invaluable feedback throughout the process. This book simply would not have been possible without her.

To all of the students, families, and staff at Coney Island Prep, who showed me what a special place a school can really be. Your undying courage and commitment to Coney Island Prep's lofty mission of preparing every student to succeed in the college and career of their choice is inspiring. I feel so honored to have been a part of the founding of the school and look forward to watching its continued success from a different perch.

I come from a family of writers and owe so much of my love of the written word to my mother, Wendy, and father, James. My mother is an incredible poet and, as I was growing up, patiently taught me how to write. She also instilled in me a life-long love of reading, for which I am eternally grateful. While parents may dream of a day when their children no longer turn to them for help with schoolwork, my parents have not been so lucky. There have been numerous times in my professional life when I have asked them for advice on an article, speech, or essay. They are always caring, giving, and thoughtful in their advice.

I'd also like to thank Paul Axtell, Cheryl McLean, Meg Gibbons, and the entire team at Sourcebooks for giving me this opportunity and for providing so much help, support, and guidance throughout the writing process.

Finally, to all those who have been a part of my getting here, particularly Molly Waxman, Kathy Batty, Leslie-Bernard Joseph, and Lindsay Freeman. And of course, Señor Amershadian and all of the other teachers along the way who never gave up on me.

About the Authors

Jacob Mnookin

Upon graduating from Middlebury College in 2002, Jacob Mnookin joined Teach For America and began his career as a professional educator at Arts High School in Newark, New Jersey.

During his time at Arts, he taught ninth and tenth grade English, served as the senior class adviser and as the faculty adviser to the National Honor Society, and coached varsity baseball.

After teaching for three years, Jacob made the

difficult decision to leave the classroom to pursue a graduate degree in public affairs at Princeton's School of Public and International Affairs. Upon graduating from Princeton, Jacob received a fellowship from Building Excellent Schools, a full-time, comprehensive training program in charter school leadership that trains individuals to design, found, and operate high-performing urban charter schools.

Jacob founded Coney Island Prep, a public charter school in Brooklyn, New York, that he ran for over ten years. The school, which opened with 90 fifth grade students and 12 staff members in 2009 in the Carey Gardens Community Center just a block from the iconic boardwalk, is a school of firsts. The first charter school in South Brooklyn, it is also the first to be run out of a public housing development. Eight years later, those original fifth graders graduated from high school with a 100% college acceptance rate, dramatically outperforming the neighborhood averages. Coney Island Prep currently serves over 1,000 students in grades K–12 with 175 staff members.

Jacob lives with his wife, Isabel, in Brooklyn, NY. Jacob currently serves as the Director of Schools for SchoolHouse and hosts the education-focused podcast *Education Tomorrow*.

PHOTO © CINDY OFFICER

Paul Axtell

Paul Axtell provides consulting and personal effectiveness training to a wide variety of clients, from Fortune 100 companies and universities to nonprofit organizations and government agencies. With an engineering degree from South Dakota School of Mines and an MBA from Washington University in St. Louis, Paul spent his early career in manufacturing, engineering, and management.

For the last twenty years, Paul's focus has been devoted to designing and leading programs that enhance individual and group performance, whether for line workers and admin staff at a manufacturing plant or regional managers and CEOs in global corporations. He has gathered decades of insights into a succinct collection of fifteen strategies in a small but powerful booklet, *Being Remarkable*. It is the centerpiece of the Being Remarkable Series, a training program complete with a facilitation guide for trainers as well as a personal workbook for individuals or small groups to work through independently. The series also includes access to Paul's video introductions to the journey toward being remarkable as well as to each strategy.

His book *Meetings Matter: 8 Powerful Strategies for Remarkable Conversations* offers a deeper dive into improving meeting competence. It won numerous awards, including the Nonfiction, Benjamin Franklin, Eric Hoffer, and Nautilus Book Awards.

A new edition of his book *Ten Powerful Things to Say to Your Kids: Creating the Relationship You Want with the Most Important People in Your Life* applies the concepts behind his work to the special relationships between parents and children of all ages.

Named Best Parenting Book of 2012, it has since been translated into Korean, Vietnamese, Chinese, Arabic, French, and Spanish.

Paul lives with his wife, Cindy, in Phoenix.

NEW! Only from Simple Truths®

IGNITE READS
spark impact in just one hour

IGNITE READS IS A NEW SERIES OF 1-HOUR READS WRITTEN BY WORLD-RENOWNED EXPERTS!

These captivating books will help you become the best version of yourself, allowing for new opportunities in your personal and professional life. Accelerate your career and expand your knowledge with these powerful books written on today's hottest ideas.

TRENDING BUSINESS AND PERSONAL GROWTH TOPICS

 Read in an hour or less

 Leading experts and authors

 Bold design and captivating content

EXCLUSIVELY AVAILABLE ON SIMPLETRUTHS.COM

Need a training framework?
Engage your team with discussion guides and PowerPoints for training events or meetings.

Want your own branded editions?
Express gratitude, appreciation, and instill positive perceptions to staff or clients by adding your organization's logo to your edition of the book.

Add a supplemental visual experience
to any meeting, training, or event.

Contact us for special corporate discounts!
(800) 900-3427 x247 or
simpletruths@sourcebooks.com

LOVED WHAT YOU READ AND WANT MORE?

Sign up today and be the FIRST to receive advance copies of Simple Truths® NEW releases written and signed by expert authors. Enjoy a complete package of supplemental materials that can help you host or lead a successful event. This high-value program will uplift you to be the best version of yourself!

— SIMPLE TRUTHS —
ELITE CLUB
ONE MONTH. ONE BOOK. ONE HOUR.

Your monthly dose of motivation, inspiration, and personal growth.